LASSIE

# Lassie

## THE EXTRAORDINARY STORY OF ERIC KNIGHT
## AND THE WORLD'S FAVOURITE DOG

### EDITED BY PETER HAINING

Peter Owen
London and Chester Springs

**PETER OWEN PUBLISHERS**
73 Kenway Road
London SW5 0RE

Peter Owen books are distributed
in the USA by
Dufour Editions Inc.,
Chester Springs,
PA 19425-0007

First published in Great Britain
by Peter Owen Publishers 2005

© Peter Haining 2006

ISBN 0 7206 1267 5

A catalogue record for this book is
available from the British Library

Printed and bound In Singapore by
Excel Print Media

*In Memory of*

**BIGGLES**
Also a female known
by a male name

# Acknowledgements

The writing of this book would not have been possible if my interest in Lassie had not been started as a child by my parents and relatives in Yorkshire. Their interest in 'the world's favourite dog' and Eric Knight, the locally born author who created Lassie and started an enduring legend, inspired me to collect material relating to collies and has resulted in this special tribute. I am also grateful to the following people for providing information, photographs, illustrations and quotes about Lassie: Pippa Miller, Chris Scott, Henry Jenkins, Alexandra Harper, Bob Weatherwax, Gayle Kaye, Eric Parker, Jeffrey M. Masson, Bob and Marcia Brown and G.F. Brazier; also the Yale Collection of American Literature, the British Newspaper Library at Colindale, the London Library, the British Film Institute, the *New York Times*, the *Des Moines Register*, the *Daily Mail*, *The Times* and *Dell Comics*.

# Contents

**Publicity poster for the 1943 film version of Eric Knight's *Lassie Come Home***

'The most popular animal ever in film' – Pal, the original screen Lassie

# CHAPTER ONE

# *Lassie — the Icon*

I N JANUARY 2002 the BBC in London announced that its viewers had voted Lassie 'the most popular animal ever in film'. The beautiful collie with her almost human-like intelligence and bravery had scored more votes than Toto, the snappy little terrier in *The Wizard of Oz*; Babe, the talking pig; and even Harry Potter's owl, Hedwig. The accolade was, in fact, just the latest in a long line of tributes and awards to the dog who has become an institution famous all over the world – and one of only two canines to be awarded a star on the Hollywood Walk of Fame (the other is Rin Tin Tin). Lassie has also undoubtedly done more for the popularity of the breed than any other single dog. No mean achievement for a fictional character created over sixty-five years ago by Eric Knight, an exiled Englishman living in America.

The story of Lassie's separation from an impoverished Yorkshire family that is forced to sell her to a Scottish nobleman and how the dog finds her way back to her young master is familiar to countless people, many of whom may not have read Eric Knight's book, seen the films or even viewed an episode of the television series that was born in the medium's black-and-white infancy and is still repeated today on cable television. The dog has become an icon, embodying the best canine virtues as well as showing a special affection for children. She has also come to symbolize the end of a time when there were divisions between the working dogs of the working class and the show dogs of the upper class, not to mention that she has promoted a real appreciation of the finest qualities of her breed.

*Lassie Come Home*, Eric Knight's story that launched this phenomenon in the dark days before the Second World War, has been described as a highly moral tale 'celebrating the faith of a boy and the redemptive power of a dog'. The name has become a synonym for loyalty, fidelity, perseverance and rescue. Equally, the book has been likened to another classic written at the same time, *How Green Was My Valley* by Richard Llewellyn, published in 1939. Both authors used sentimental realism to raise public awareness about the plight of the British working class – in particular the mining areas where employment was in steady decline – and both men were driven by a desire for social reform.

Henry Jenkins, an American social historian, has examined the appeal of Lassie in some detail, especially on television. Writing in an essay, 'The Sentimental Value of Lassie' (1994), he says:

> Many animal series saw their non-human protagonists as playful, mischievous and child-like, leading their owners into scrapes, then helping them get out again. Lassie, however, was consistently portrayed as highly responsible, caring and nurturing. In so far as she created problems for her owners, they were problems

caused by her eagerness to help others, a commitment to a community larger than the family, and more often her role was to rescue those in peril and to set right wrongs that had been committed. She was the perfect 'mother' as defined within the 1950s and 1960s. American ideology, ironically, of course – the dogs who have played Lassie through the years have all been male.

**A 'rough collie' – the inspiration for Lassie**

The sex of Lassie is not the only misconception that has become attached to the legend of Lassie. Indeed, from the first time the public developed a fascination with collies in the Victorian era, by way of Eric Knight's original short-story version of *Lassie Come Home* in the *Saturday Evening Post* and on to the Lassie films, radio and television programmes, one erroneous belief has followed another – in particular the dog's type, her characteristics and her nature.

Lassie is not a 'shepherd dog', as she has all too often been categorized, but a 'rough collie' of a type originally used to guard sheep and cattle in pastures. She is quite distinct from the smooth collie – sometimes referred to in Scotland as the 'ban' dog because it does not have the flowing coat of its cousin – used to guide cows and sheep to market. Although all the collies used in the films and on television have had a distinctive white blaze on their foreheads, the author's original is actually described as having 'a perfect black mask' similar to that seen in dogs in the villages and moors of Yorkshire and Scotland. The characteristics of the male and female rough collies also differ: the males are bigger than the females, have thicker coats and retain this fullness when moulting. Film-makers have always chosen to use the bigger, more 'heroic-looking' male dogs as their supposedly female star. As for the idea that collies are by nature loyal and affectionate, the original Lassie, a dog named Pal, had a tendency to chase motor cycles and very nearly lost his trainer the most coveted animal role in Hollywood.

Queen Victoria is credited with starting the public interest in rough collies, and there have been a number of famous owners among the millions who have subsequently owned the dogs. The author Jerome K. Jerome (1859–1927) had a pair which he described as 'sitting patient, good and thoughtful' despite being annoyed by a yapping fox terrier similar to the one that featured in *Three Men in a Boat*; while the Antarctic explorer Captain Robert Scott (1868–1912) mentions in his *Last Expedition* the bravery of a collie who gave birth to six puppies during their hazardous journey. The bitch, incidentally, was named Lassie.

My own interest in the Lassie story stems from childhood. I was the son of

parents who were both born in Yorkshire within a short distance of the setting of *Lassie Come Home*, and they introduced me to the book as a child. In my early teens I also enjoyed the films, followed by the early years of the television series. More recently, my own children have got great pleasure from watching the series in later repeats in the 1970s and 1980s.

Throughout all this time Lassie has, of course, grown as a popular hero, and

**Lassie to the rescue in
*Lassie and the Mystery
of Blackberry Bog*,
illustrated by Ken Sawyer**

**An early issue of Dell Comic's *Lassie* (April 1951)**

her image has been used widely in the media and in merchandising of all kinds. The early films, such as *Challenge to Lassie* (1949), were adapted into picture books for children with stills and colour pictures.

In the 1950s the US publishers Whitman Publishing of Wisconsin launched a series of titles based on the television programmes with titles such as *Lassie and the Mystery of the Blackberry Bog* by Dorothea J. Snow and *Lassie: Trouble at Panter's Lake* by Steve Frazee, all colourfully illustrated by Ken Sawyer.

Manufacturers in America and Britain released a plethora of souvenirs to cater to the public fascination with Lassie. These items ranged from china models to wrist watches, jigsaw puzzles, lunch boxes and even a blow-up toy, 'Lassie – Wonder Dog of TV'. This was a phenomenon that would certainly have astonished the dog's modest creator if he had lived long enough to witness even a small fraction of this Lassie-mania.

One of Lassie's most gorgeous co-stars, the cartoon character Gerry

Like many others of my generation growing up in the 1950s, I enjoyed the American comic books that crossed the Atlantic in bulk containers and were often sold cheaply in chain stores such as Woolworth's. Dell Publishing in New York issued *Lassie*, a monthly colour cartoon-strip magazine that offered a more adventurous and exciting storyline than the films or television series and was clearly intended to appeal to adolescents. Their Lassie belonged to a lively young couple, Rocky and his girlfriend Gerry (whom he later married), who were employed to investigate and write about historic locations in exotic parts of South America. Whenever they got into trouble – which happened in every issue – encountering illicit explorers, illegal big-game hunters, smugglers, pirates or any number of other assorted villains, Lassie would invariably play a major role in rescuing them and bringing the bad guys to justice.

The archetypal blond-haired, square-jawed, all-American guy, Rocky had less impact on our youthful senses than the gorgeous Gerry with her swathe of black hair and pretty face who was never far away from the centre of the action. She was somewhat ahead of her time, too, often wearing shorts that showed off her shapely legs, exposing her midriff and revealing a hint of cleavage. To my contemporaries, she became one of our first pin-ups – even if she was merely a colour sketch .

All of these elements played a part in making Lassie the most famous dog in the world. It was the progeny of Pal who played the original on screen – all belonging to the same trainer, Rudd Weatherwax – that have ensured the perpetuation of the canine legend. When not filming, each of these nine collies has gone on promotional tours or made celebrity appearances at dog shows and obedience and agility trials. This book acknowledges their contribution, that of the breed to which they all belong and especially Eric Knight, the author without whose inspiration none of this would have happened.

It was the famous eighteenth-century Scottish poet Robbie Burns, himself the owner of a rough collie, Luath, who composed some lines on his dog's 'honest, sonsie, bawsint face / aye gat him friends in ilka place'. 'Sonsie', I should explain to those not familiar with the Scottish dialect, means open, happy and engaging, while a 'bawsint face' is one with a bold white blaze. This definition, it seems to me, still fits the descendants of the collie almost a century and a half after Burns wrote his immortal lines.

SHEPHERD OR COLLIE DOG

Postcard marking the founding of the Collie Club of America in 1886

# CHAPTER TWO

# Queen Victoria's Favourite Dog

A SCOTTISH CLERGYMAN and amateur historian, Alexander Stewart, claimed in an article written in 1889 that the collie was 'the oldest indigenous dog of the British Isles'. Furthermore, said the fervent dog-lover writing in the *Live Stock Journal*, he believed that the breed had been one of mankind's closest companions for thousands of years. 'Fingal's dog, Bran, was just an exceptionally strong and intelligent collie,' he wrote, 'and it would not be hard to persuade me that the faithful Argus of Ulysses in far-off Ithaca, three thousand years ago, was any other than a genuine collie of the same breed as the Fingalian's more than a thousand years afterwards in the hunting grounds of medieval Scotland and Ireland.'

It may be a little difficult to believe that the faithful Argus, who waited patiently for twenty years for his master to return and then died with a last wag of his tail at seeing him again, was a collie – but the breed *is* very ancient. And Argus's sense of devotion and loyalty to his master is undoubtedly in a direct line of canine history leading to the modern odyssey of Lassie. Contemporary social historian Marjorie Garber draws the same comparison in her book *Dog Love* (1997): 'Lassie is not only the faithful Argus, waiting at home for her master, but also the quest hero Odysseus (or Ulysses), crossing a fearful and unknown territory in search of home and love.'

There are other historians who have suggested the collie may be a descendant of the dogs brought to Britain by the Roman invaders before the time of Christ. Their argument is that around 50 BC these animals from southern climes interbred with the hardy Scottish dogs, resulting in the handsome, robust breed that gradually populated the northern parts of the island.

Be that as it may, there is no doubt the collie is of ancient lineage. The name is believed to have been derived from 'coalie' or 'coaly', a term used to describe the mountain sheep with black faces and feet known by these names which the dogs herded. Alternatively, it could refer to their own predominantly black colour. A further school of thought has suggested that collie and 'col' may be from the same root as 'collar' because of the white collar around the animal's neck – although it has to be said that 'col' is also an Anglo-Saxon word for black.

Despite this long tradition, however, there are actually few references to the collie in literature. Geoffrey Chaucer is one of the few exceptions, writing in 1387 about 'Coll our dog'. There is a short section about the breed in a Renaissance folio, *De Canibus Britannicis* (*Of Englishe Dogges*) by Dr John Caius, a Humanist, physician and co-founder of the Cambridge University college that bears his name. The book, written in Latin in 1570 and not translated into English until seven years later, categorizes the collie among shepherd dogs and describes it as 'a goode herd dogge for sheepe and cattel'. Not until a hundred years later was the

**Engraving of a collie, 1653**

first engraving of a collie published in an anonymous pamphlet featuring dogs, dated 1653.

By the eighteenth century the Scottish collie was widely recognized as one of the best sheepdogs in the world. Oliver Goldsmith, the intemperate novelist, essayist and author of the classic play *She Stoops to Conquer* (1773), whose ramshackle life might have left him little time for interest in animals, reinforced this view in one of his articles, where he wrote that the collie was 'of all dogs the most intelligent and faithful and at the same time the most useful'. Other admirers claimed that the collie had equal qualities of sight, hearing and scent. Some of the dogs were said to have the 'wall eye' which farmers held to be a great advantage as it allowed the dogs to focus on distant objects with the lighter-coloured eye and on nearer ones with the darker eye. Patricia Dale-Green discusses these qualities in her book *Dog* (1966):

> Much of the collie's capacity for herding and rounding up livestock is inherent and it shows great eagerness to learn. Collie puppies are stimulated by the sight of sheep at ten weeks old, before they have either seen older dogs working or received any training. At a very early age they will stalk and try to herd anything that moves, including lambs, chicks, ducklings, insects and even ripples on a pond. They stare intently at the objects of their interest – behaviour known as 'showing eye' which develops into one of the main techniques used by adult dogs for controlling their flocks. Collies must be capable of great speed and endurance, have active resourceful brains and temperaments, and be calm enough to enable them to work flocks without producing panic. The training of collies depends on the quality, intelligence and inherited gifts of the individual and the patience of the trainer.

In the middle of the nineteenth century dog fanciers throughout the British Isles began to take a real interest in the collie. The first breeding programmes were initiated, and some of the best collies were brought to county fairs to be exhibited as show dogs rather than just working animals. It was at one of these shows in Scotland that the story of the collie changed for ever. According to historian Cecil G. Trew in *The Story of the Dog* (1940), at this time the breed was little known outside Scotland, parts of the north of England and the mountainous areas of Wales. Until, that is, Royalty suddenly became interested in collies:

> In 1860, Queen Victoria, on a visit to her estate at Balmoral in Scotland, was so impressed with the beauty and intelligence of the collie that she brought one home with her to the royal kennels in Windsor Castle. This stimulated public interest and, as is always the case, considerable changes were brought about, until to-day the show collie and the working collie are practically considered to be separate breeds.

Alexandra, Princess of Wales, was also caught up in the Queen's enthusiasm for the breed and established her own kennels. Her particular interest was for the rough-coated collies that she had seen on visits to Wales and during stays in Scotland. Towards the end of the century the Princess began exhibiting her best animals, and in 1900 her rough collie Lochiel – named after the area of Scotland from which the animal had originated – was a prize-winner at a show in London.

This victory gave the seal of approval to rough collies as far as the general public were concerned. The breed had, though, been exciting interest among fanciers since 1867 when a dog named Old Cockie was born. He was the first with the original sable coloration associated with rough collies, and it has been claimed that most collies of this type have Old Cockie in their lineage. Less than a

ROUGH·COLLIE "LOCHIEL"· H.R.H. PRINCESS ᴏꜰ WALES·OWNER.

decade later, in 1873, a dog was whelped named Trefoil with black, white and golden sable colouring – and the tricolour collie, of which the screen Lassie is the most famous example, came into existence. The first example to enter a show-ring made his début a few years later at the Birmingham Dog Society Show.

Because of these changes and an obvious need for standards the Collie Club was established in 1881, and four years later it was accepted into the English Kennel Club. The new organization became the forerunner of several more clubs – including the Collie Club of America, founded in 1886 – all intent on 'promoting the breeding of true collies and a recognized and unvarying type'. By a strange quirk of fate one of the earliest dogs to be used to illustrate the ideal rough-coated collie was Carlyle, sired by Perthshire Bob out of Old Lassie. He was sketched in 1894 by permission of his owner, the aptly named Dr W.A.G. James.

The first President of the Collie Club was the Reverend Hans F. Hamilton of Woodmansterne in Surrey, who is referred to in contemporary accounts as 'the foster-father of the breed'. He was responsible for writing the first detailed definition of a rough collie in 1904, thereby providing a yardstick for the future:

The rough collie of the present day has developed into a creature of great beauty and symmetrical form. He is the most sagacious, useful and striking of all dogs, and is evolved from the rougher specimens that existed long ago and are still to be seen in many places. The head is considerably lengthened and well chiselled; the ears placed rather high on the head and carried ordinarily so as to be hardly seen as they lie back in the long hair behind them. But when interested or excited they are raised to a half-cock, with the tip falling forwards at the points. The eyes should be almond-shaped and set obliquely in the head; in colour any shade of brown, only not too light, nor too prominent, but bright and piercing. The skin tight and the hair short all over the head and the whole expression full of kindliness, brightness and intelligence.

The neck must be set becomingly and lightly on well-shaped, sloping shoulders; the chest deep and rather broad; the back long and free from hollowness; the fore legs straight and well-feathered; the hind legs sinewy to afford

ROUGH-COATED COLLIE.

Dr. W. A. G. James' CARLYLE (K.C.S.B., 8505). Sire, Perthshire Bob, by Bob of Rug, out of Cloudy ; Dam, Mr. Jones' Old Lassie.

plenty of propelling power; the tail carried gracefully without a twist, although raised high when excited. There is a double coat, the outside one being straight and free from woolliness; but beneath there is an undergrowth which covers the skin and protects the wearer from cold and wet. The size depends much on feeding and bringing up and having no drawbacks in the shape of illness to take away from the raciness so essential to the discharge of duties devolving on the dog, which render it necessary that he should be lithe, active and agile and built on galloping lines and possessed of staying power.

The President concluded his statement, 'The rough collie is aristocratic in appearance and full of grace and so beautiful that people turn to notice him as he passes on his way and say admiringly, "Look at that lovely dog!" He is, indeed, beautiful to look upon, charming as a companion and the best of guards.'

The Reverend Hamilton was also a very successful breeder and in 1898 reared a rough-coated collie Sefton Hero, which fetched the then highest price ever paid for a collie of £1,200. Writing about the record figure in *The Twentieth Century Dog* (1904), Herbert Compton noted resignedly, 'The collie went to America – where all good dogs go!'

When he wrote this, Compton could have had no idea how prescient his words would prove in the history of the rough collie – and of one dog in particular . . .

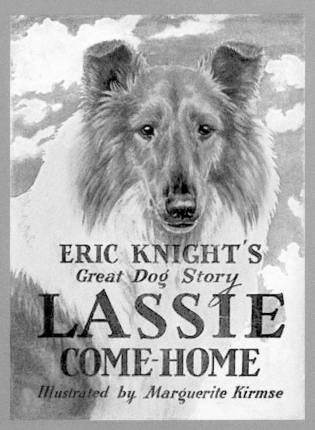

ERIC KNIGHT'S
*Great Dog Story*
LASSIE
COME-HOME
*Illustrated by Marguerite Kirmse*

An early American edition of Eric Knight's book (published by
John C. Winston, Philadelphia, 1940)

# CHAPTER THREE

# The Collie's Homing Instinct

THERE HAVE BEEN a number of extraordinary true stories of lost or aban-doned dogs finding their way home after travelling great distances, as typified in *Lassie Come Home*. These reunions have all posed the same question: What unique ability do the animals possess to enable them successfully to complete this journey, alongside purpose, resilience and unwavering deter-mination? It is a question that has intrigued many owners, breeders, vets and scientists both before and since Eric Knight created the most famous fictional account of one collie's 'homing' instinct.

This ability is not confined to collies, and there are stories from the past two centuries of travel feats by a variety of dogs ranging from red setters to poodles. Per-haps the most famous of these is the rather shamefaced account by the great French writer Victor Hugo (1802–85) concerning his poodle Baron. Hugo was the author of the panoramic tale of social injustice *Les Misérables* (1862), with its memorable monologue by the liberated convict Jean Valjean, 'I went into a dog's kennel; the dog bit me and chased me off, as though he had been a man.' Hugo was a dog-lover all his life. He had a special fondness for poodles, celebrated in his poem 'Chelles'.

# LASSIE

The Frenchman's most agonizing experience occurred when he was visiting Moscow in 1872. According to a letter to a friend collected in *Oeuvres Complètes de Victor Hugo* (1961), on the spur of the moment he gave Baron away to a Russian count who had expressed great admiration for the dog. Hugo left the city a week later, already beginning to regret his decision. 'To my astonishment,' he informed his friend, 'some months later, Baron, alone, but determined, walked from the count's country house outside Moscow to Paris. There was a joyful reunion for us both and my remorse at what I did is inexcusable.' The hardships and hunger the dog must have endured crossing that vast continent and over much of Europe can only be imagined – rather like those of an Irish red setter, Dinah, the following century. Although the distance involved was shorter, as R.H. Smythe reports in his book *The Mind of the Dog* (1919), the bitch was about to give birth:

> Dinah was sent from Cookstown to Lurgan, a matter of twenty-five miles, by train. Shortly after her arrival, she whelped five puppies, and then promptly disappeared from her new home, puppies and all. Ten days later she was found at Cookstown asleep in her old nest with the five puppies, all alive and healthy, tucked in alongside her. Her feet were raw and bleeding and she was dreadfully emaciated. She had obviously travelled on foot and must have transported the five puppies in relays of short distance, so how many times she actually covered the mileage is unknown. On her way she swam, complete with family, the River Blackwater at Mahery Ferry, where it is over eighty yards wide and very deep, a

number of times in each direction, leaving some of her puppies on the opposite shore to await her return while she fetched more. Dinah recovered, reared all her puppies, and remained a resident of Cookstown for the remainder of her days.

Other stories of homing dogs refer to their having found their way back by travelling along roads, while a few have even boarded trains, buses or boats that they inexplicably knew were going to the right destination. Collies, in particular, have a special affection for where they live, as *Lassie Come Home* demonstrates. An earlier collie owner, the barrister-turned-essayist Walter Herries Pollock (1850–1926), provided a particularly good example of this in a story about his much-loved rough collie Douglas. It appears in his delightfully entitled memoirs *Animals That Have Owned Us* (1920), in which he describes Douglas's 'humour, memory and knowledge of the meaning of the word home' and recalls a vivid example that could almost have inspired an episode in Eric Knight's book:

> Like most dogs of mark, he always knew when we were going away and when we were coming back and he resented exceedingly the signs of our departure. On one occasion when the work of packing had been well begun, I heard a cry of dismay from my wife. On rushing up to see what was the matter, I found Douglas still busily engaged in the half-accomplished task of shovelling all her carefully arranged dresses out of a trunk with his nose and forepaws – a performance for which it was impossible to scold him.

Walter Herries Pollock's home-loving collie Douglas, described in *Animal's That Have Owned Us* (1920)

# THE COLLIE'S HOMING INSTINCT

There is a real-life precedent to *Lassie Come Home* in the amazing journey of Bobbie, a three-year-old collie that belonged to an American farmer Frank Brazier. In 1924 the animal became known as 'the wonder dog of Oregon' after a six-month cross-country trek of 2,551 miles to be reunited with his owner. The event became something of a sensation in America after it was reported in the local and national papers. Sensationalized versions in books and magazines, as well as a feature in the syndicated column about natural phenomena, 'Ripley's Believe It or Not', followed these accounts. There was even a film, *Bobbie the Wonder Dog*, in which he appeared. In the retelling the story perhaps inevitably became distorted, with the addition of a number of incidents that were total invention. However, I have discovered an article written at the time by Frank Brazier for a limited-circulation magazine, *Animal Pals*, which will help to set the record straight.

Frank and his wife Elizabeth and their two daughters Nova and Leona had just moved to the Abiqua region of Oregon from Indiana and bought a six-week-old collie puppy they had named Bobbie. The Braziers already owned a fox terrier, Toodles, who quickly made friends with the lively newcomer as the family set about making a new life for themselves. Frank explains:

> We all worked in the hop fields, both dogs playing near and having the time of their lives. We moved often, following the market demands, and very soon Bobbie began to show aptitudes that were to stand him in good stead later. He was a natural 'heeler.' When only two months old he would heel cats, horses and people,

driving them ahead of him wherever he wanted them to go. At one place he was bringing in a horse who was lively with his hoofs, and before Bobbie knew it he was sailing through the air with a well-placed kick. He blinked and caught his breath and the next second was up and after the rebellious equine, keeping at a safe distance, but pursuing him until he was safe in the corral. This left a mark over the dog's eye which helped to identify him at a future date.

Our next stop was a fruit farm where they used a tractor. Bobbie was asleep, quite unconscious of danger, when the machine caught him. His leg was crushed into the ground, which, fortunately, being deeply cultivated, was very soft and kept him from serious injury, but the mishap left another scar. His third accident came from an encounter with an old gopher. While digging furiously to get at the 'vermin' he broke off parts of two teeth.

If Bobbie seemed destined for a long if dangerous life, the Braziers' other pet dog was not so lucky. Just after the collie reached his first birthday, Toodles had a stroke and died. Already growing disillusioned with the farming life, the family decided to make another career change – purchasing a café, the Reo Lunch Restaurant, in Silverton. However, they decided that the environment was probably not a good one for a dog used to the open countryside and sold Bobbie to a farmer friend. At once the collie began to display his homing instinct by appearing at the café each weekend – and had to be returned to his new owner each Monday morning.

After they had run the busy restaurant for several months, Frank and his wife decided to take a break and visit some old friends back in Indiana. Missing Bobbie, too, Frank went to buy his dog back. 'So we repurchased him at three times the amount we had sold him for and, one fine morning, left Silverton in our touring car, the dog riding on the running board or on top of the luggage. How that dog enjoyed the trip! When we were going slow enough or stopped for a bite to eat he would dash off after a rabbit or on an exploring expedition over the hills, coming back after an hour or so, panting and grinning to tell us all about it!'

The couple made their first stop in Indiana at the small town of Wolcott on 15 August. While Frank was refuelling his car, Bobbie was set upon by three local dogs and disappeared round the corner of the filling station. Although Frank expected his collie to return, as the hours passed and there was no sign he grew increasingly concerned. Even driving around the town sounding his horn – a signal that normally brought Bobbie running – failed to bring him back.

There was still no sign of the collie the following day. After placing an advertisement in the local weekly paper appealing for the return of Bobbie, Frank and Elizabeth continued touring around Indiana for the next three weeks, hoping against hope that when they returned to Wolcott Bobbie might have been found. Their hopes were dashed, however, and, saddened that they had probably lost their pet for ever, the Braziers drove back to Oregon. Six months passed, Frank recalled, and they had almost forgotten the lively collie when something totally unexpected happened:

**Bobbie who travelled over 2,500 miles to be reunited with his owner Frank Brazier**

My youngest girl, Nova, and her chum were walking down a street in Silverton when suddenly my daughter gasped and seized her friend by the arm, exclaiming, 'Oh, look, isn't that Bobbie?' At the words a shaggy, bedraggled, lean dog just beyond them turned his head and the next moment fairly flew at Nova, leaping up again and again to cover her face with kisses and making half-strangled, sobbing sounds of relief and delight as if he could hardly voice his wordless joy. It was Bobbie, sure enough, and it was a glad and triumphant procession which hurried on to the restaurant, where the dog hunted out my wife and Leona and told them how happy he was to be home again.

Frank, who was asleep upstairs, was awoken by the commotion below him, and moments later Bobbie bounded into the bedroom and was licking him affectionately. Only when his shock at this amazing reappearance had passed did Frank realize that the date was 15 February 1924, six months to the very day since had had last seen the collie . . . over 2,500 miles away. It was no surprise, as he wrote later, that the dog was 'all in':

> For three days, Bobbie did little but eat and sleep and would look at us so pitifully as if to say, 'My, but I am just worn out. Can't you help me?' He would roll over on his back and hold up his pads, fixing us with his eyes to tell us how sore his feet were. His toenails were down to the quick, his eyes inflamed, his coat uneven and matted and his whole bearing that of an animal which had been through a grilling experience. When he first came back, he would eat little but raw meat, showing that he had depended for sustenance chiefly on his own catches of rabbits or prairie fowl.

If any member of Frank Brazier's family doubted for even a moment that it was the same Bobbie that had returned home, any such misgivings were dispelled when they revisited the farm where they previously lived. No sooner had they reached the site than the collie immediately ran to the spot where the fox terrier

Toodles was buried. With tears stinging his ears, Frank had to gently pull away Bobbie before he could excavate the bones of his former friend.

On 23 February 1924 the *Silverton Appeal* ran a story headlined 'Dog Returns After Long Trip' and began the escalation of the legend. The achievement, the paper said, 'demonstrates a remarkable instinct or reasoning power as one chooses to call it'. As the story spread further afield, the Braziers were soon receiving letters from people who had seen Bobbie on his long journey, some of whom had apparently housed and fed him before he moved on across rivers, over prairies and sometimes even into towns, always heading for Silverton. It was evident, too, that he must have made essential detours, which probably pushed the total distance covered to nearer 3,000 miles – all through the depths of winter. As Frank added, 'We were told he was always looking for someone and always in a hurry.'

Bobbie's feat of homing is now acknowledged as the furthest distance ever travelled by a collie – and most other breeds, too – and it was one of the elements that sparked research during the 1930s by Professor Basian Schmid (1870–1944), a German animal behaviour researcher in Munich. Schmid carried out a series of elaborate experiments on the ability of dogs to find their way home and concluded that 'neither scent nor vision is involved'. The Professor felt there had to be an unknown factor involved that 'should perhaps be called an absolute sense of orientation'. Such dogs were probably driven by love for their owner, Schmid said, adding that there was also the possibility of '*heimweh* [homepain], a feeling of homesickness similar to that experienced by human beings'.

This love of canines for their owners is also considered by Jeffrey M. Masson in his recent book *Dogs Never Lie About Love* (1997), in which he complains about the paucity of research into the subject. 'Veterinarians have no clue as to what sense are involved in this homing instinct,' he writes. 'Certainly smell and visual clues are critical, but beyond that, could there be a sense completely unknown to us that dogs are able to call into play? What enables some dogs to find their way back over vast distances while others are forever getting lost a

block from their homes? Here is an area where experiments could easily be conducted, without putting the dog under great stress, by simply making the test a game.'

The story of Bobbie, 'The Wonder of Oregon', also attracted the interest of the author Albert Payson Terhune (1872–1942) who during the 1920s and 1930s was the most prolific writer of collie books in America. A devoted breeder, trainer and owner of collies,

**American author Albert Payson Terhune and his favourite collie Lad**

Terhune wrote more than a dozen novels about them – including several about his own favourite dogs Lad, Bruce, Wolf and Gray Dawn – which 'created a spark of love for dogs in general and for collies in particular', according to the *Dog Owner's Guide* (2002).

Terhune spent his life at the home where he had been born, Sunnybank, on the shores of Lake Pompton in New Jersey, and, although noted for his complex and eccentric nature, he delighted millions with his prodigious output of collie books that were largely set in America, with the occasional significant foray to Scotland in *Lochinvar Luck* (1923) and *A Highland Collie* (1927). He immortalized Lad, his first collie, born in 1902, 'a hero of d'Artagnan-like stature', in three volumes, *Lad: A Dog* (1919), *Further Adventures of Lad* (1922) and *Lad of Sunnybank* (1929). In a later biographical note in *Some Sunnybank Dogs* (1937) Terhune wrote of his great favourite:

> He was a big and incredibly powerful collie with a massive coat of burnished mahogany-and-snow and with absurdly small forepaws (which he spent at least an hour a day in washing) and with deepest dark eyes that seemed to have a soul behind them. So much for the outer dog. For the inner: he had a heart that did not know the meaning of fear or disloyalty or of meanness. But it was his personality, apart from all these things, which made – and still makes him – so impossible to forget. He was immeasurably more than a professionally loyal and heroic collie. He had the elfin sense of fun and the most humanlike reasoning powers I have found in any dog.

One of Diana Thorne's beautiful collies from *The Dog Book* (1932)

Such indeed was the impact of Lad on readers that ever since the author's death collie fanciers have travelled to Sunnybank Farm each year to pay tribute to his memory. The dog's last resting place in the grounds is marked by a marble stone bearing the words 'Lad – Thoroughbred in Body and Soul', and apart from acknowledging the dog who 'brought national fame to the breed and opened the eyes of thousands of children to the potential for a close relationship with a dog' the gathering also raises money to support research into breed health.

A number of Terhune's books were illustrated by the brilliant Canadian artist Diana Thorne, who became acknowledged as one of the finest illustrators of collies. A resourceful young woman who had been imprisoned by the Germans while studying art in Berlin during the First World War, she had managed to escape to London where she supported herself as a librarian and began sketching animals. Moving to New York, she was soon much in demand as an illustrator for books of animal life, dogs in particular. Later the best of her pictures were assembled as *Diana Thorne's Dog Basket* (1930) – introduced with fulsome praise by Terhune – *The Dog Book* (1932) and *Diana Thorne's Dogs II* (1944), all of which are now highly collectable.

However, it was two books in particular by Albert Payson Terhune that revealed his fascination with the homing instinct: *Real Tales of Real Dogs* (1935), which contains a chapter on 'Bobbie, the Three Thousand Mile Collie', and *A Book of Famous Dogs* (1937), with an entire section devoted to 'Dogs That Travelled Far'. Like everyone else, he was unable to pinpoint why and how dogs achieved these feats beyond their desire to seek 'the scenes of earlier happiness and a great affection for their owners'.

Such was the popularity of Terhune's series of collie novels that it seems unlikely Eric Knight had not read one or more of them – or, at the very least, as a journalist, *heard* about them – when he wrote *Lassie Come Home* in 1938. He might even have come across Victor Hugo's story of Baron or the amazing exploits of Bobbie, the name of whose fox terrier friend, Toodles, was very similar to that chosen by Knight for his own dog, Toots.

In all probability, though, a greater influence on his famous story was a much older book he had read many years before as a child growing up on the other side of the Atlantic in England. This was a book by a Scottish shepherd that also featured the remarkable courage and devotion of a collie bitch . . .

Eric Knight, the creator of Lassie, photographed in 1940

# CHAPTER FOUR

# A Yorkshire Lad's Odyssey

THERE IS A story told in the village of Bewerley on the edge of the Yorkshire Moors that Eric Knight drew the inspiration for *Lassie Come Home* from the shepherd dogs he saw working flocks of sheep and a book that belonged to his temperamental uncle Vernon Creasser, the local haulier. The area is indeed famous for its hardy dogs – or 'tykes', as the local people often call them – and Creasser was certainly a man who enjoyed reading, in particular, the works of James Hogg (1770–1835), the Scottish poet and novelist, known far and wide as the 'Ettrick Shepherd'.

Vernon Creasser lived in a modest house on Bewerley's main street, where he kept a small shelf of books in the living-room that the young Eric explored through during his formative years. Among these were several volumes by Hogg, who lived a hard life in Ettrick in the wild border country of Selkirkshire tending sheep and dabbling in farming before he became a successful writer. The fact that the Scot received only a spasmodic education and had his head filled with local legends recounted to him by his mother before making his own way in the world was a mirror of Creasser's own struggle to succeed by carting goods

**A portrait of Lassie and shepherd Jock Gray, both inspired by James Hogg, the 'Ettrick Shepherd'**

around the West Riding of Yorkshire. Even the landscapes of hills, moors and forest land in which both men grew up were very similar.

The little group of titles by James Hogg in Creasser's house probably included the *Border Minstrelsy* (1803), containing several of his best poems and his tribute to Robert Burns, 'The Author's Address to His Auld Dog Hector', in which he revealed his own love of collies; *Private Memoirs and Confessions of a Justified Sinner* (1824), with its haunting portrait of a split personality; and *The Shepherd's Calendar* (1829), a mixture of rural fact and fable that some experts believe contributed to the author's soubriquet as 'the King of the Mountain and Fairy School'. There is, however, nothing fanciful but a great deal of real courage and devotion in Hogg's story 'Duncan Campbell; or, The Faithful Dog'. Young Eric Knight could hardly have failed to be moved by this tale of a shepherd and his 'colley'.

Hogg describes the hard life led by Campbell, who owned a collie bitch that he had grown to trust to leave on her own to look after his sheep, certain that she would follow his daily routine exactly. One day the dog did not appear with the flock at the usual hour, and Campbell, surprised and annoyed at this apparent lapse of duty, set out to look for her. Just a short distance from his home he found the collie driving the sheep, carrying a newborn pup in her mouth.

The shepherd was amazed at how the collie had managed to keep control of the sheep while whelping, Hogg continued, but as soon as she saw her master take charge of the flock she deposited the puppy safely and headed straight back into the hills. For the next few hours the mother went back and forth, returning each time with a puppy until she had retrieved her whole litter from several miles away. Only one of the pups failed to survive.

If the tradition in Bewerley is to be believed, Eric Knight never forgot this story when the course of his life took him from poverty in Yorkshire to a more than comfortable existence and fame in America. It might, though, have been all so different for the Yorkshire lad but for a stroke of fate that was to deal him both great success and premature tragedy.

Although Eric grew up in Bewerley, he was born on 10 April 1897 some fifteen miles to the south in the town of Menston. Situated in a lovely part of Wharfedale on the slope of Ilkley Moor, the community stands on an ancient route that linked Roman York to Preston. It was the seat of the wealthy Fairfax family and developed rapidly in the Victorian era with the opening of a rail link to the industrial city of

Leeds and the building of a large mental hospital, High Royds Hospital. (This was recently featured in the television drama *Black Daisies for the Bride* by Tony Harrison, which dealt movingly with sufferers from Alzheimer's disease and won the 1994 Italia Prize.)

Eric Mowbray Knight was the third son of Frederick Harrison Knight and Marion Hilda Creasser, both devoted Quakers. His father was a wholesale jeweller and diamond merchant who had prospered in business, and the family lived well and were used to going on exotic foreign trips – until disaster struck. Knight senior had made many contacts in the diamond industry, and in 1899 he suddenly deserted the family and moved to the source of his wealth, South Africa. He was killed, just a few months later, when the Boer War enveloped the country.

The family finances were severely depleted by the departure of Frederick Knight, and his wife was forced to seek work. With her genteel manners and experience of child-rearing, she obtained a position as a governess to the family of Princess Xenia in the Russian Royal Palace in St Petersburg. However, she decided against taking her four sons, Edmund, Frederick, Eric and the youngest, Noel, with her, and each was sent to a different relative in West Yorkshire. Eric found himself with Uncle Creasser in Bewerley, and for the rest of his life he carried vivid memories of the village and the struggles of its strong, patient and virtuous working-class people. They became one of his great concerns and would frequently appear in his later articles, stories and books.

Bewerley, which is situated on the opposite bank of the River Nidd to Pateley

Bewerley

Bridge – a tourist attraction often described as one of the loveliest spots in the Yorkshire Dales – also has its own beauties. Mentioned in the Domesday Book, the village stands in the shadow of Guise Cliff and the mock ruins known as Yorke's Folly that rise 1,000 feet above sea level. The waterfalls, woods, glens and moors that are home to great flocks of sheep all combined to make it an idyllic place for a young boy to grow up in and explore, and Eric later claimed that his time here was 'one of the happiest periods of my life'.

There was, however, a darker side to existence in Bewerley at the end of the

**Collies and sheep in the Yorkshire Dales, _c._ 1909**

Victorian era, as Eric discovered when his uncle sent him to Bewerley Bridge-housegate School on Greenhow Hill. The 200-year-old school occupied what had formerly been three cottages, and for years the Taylor family, who had grown rich as owners of the local lead mines, had paid the salary of the schoolmaster. Despite his own privileged background, Eric was utterly captivated by the speech patterns and behaviour of the other children and appalled at the harsh lives of many of their fathers in the mines. He took to roaming the fields and moors where he first set eyes on the working collies which were so vital to Yorkshire shepherds, as Susan M. Brown has observed in her booklet *Lassie: A Collie and Her Influence* (1993):

> The collie enjoyed a dual status in British culture: on the one hand, the breed was the favourite of Queen Victoria, closely associated with the aristocracy and highly valued as a show dog among the breeders; on the other hand, the collie was an excellent work dog, especially good at herding . . . You can go into any one of the hundreds of small mining villages in this largest of England's counties [Yorkshire] and see, walking at the heels of humbly clad workmen, dogs of such a fine breed and aristocratic bearing as to arouse the envy of wealthier dog fanciers from other parts of the world.

As Eric Knight trekked across the hills around his home such pictures must have become permanently ingrained on his mind. It was at this time, too, that he first began to develop a talent for drawing and sketching. Among his effects from

**One of the wooden collie dogs carved by Eric Knight**

this period is an early sketchbook containing a number of animal studies and portraits of various Yorkshire characters that he obviously encountered on these walks. He also made his first little wooden models of collies – a pastime that later became something of a passion – and there are clues that he dreamed of becoming an artist one day.

As far as Knight's general education was concerned, as with so many of his contemporaries in the poorer areas of England, it came to a halt as soon as he reached the age of twelve. There was little work for boys in Bewerley apart from the mines, so Eric had no alternative but to look for a job in nearby Leeds.

In 1909 he became a 'bobbin doffer' in one of the city's large woollen mills. He soon grew tired of the laborious work and the lint that flew about, getting into everyone's lungs. During the next three years he worked in an engineering plant, a sawmill and a glass factory. The conditions in all of these places were terrible: the workers were forced to put in long hours for minimum wages and could be laid off at a moment's notice when demand for any product fell. Young Eric developed a great affinity with his fellow labourers and took part in at least one strike seeking better working conditions.

Eric might easily have fallen into the pattern of a grinding and unrewarding life, but things changed suddenly in 1912. His mother Marion, who in the interim had given up her job in Russia and emigrated to the USA where she had married an American, wrote asking him to join her. The same invitation was extended to Edmund and Frederick, who were also at work in Yorkshire. Tragically, the youngest son, Noel, had died in infancy. The family was reunited in Philadelphia in the autumn of that year.

For the first time, fifteen-year-old Eric was able to get a job that better suited his artistic tendencies, working as a copy boy on the *Philadelphia Press*. His mother, though, was keen that he should further his education, and he was sent back to school, first to the Cambridge Latin School in Massachusetts, then the Boston Museum of Fine Arts School and finally the National Academy of Design in New York. His burgeoning talent was recognized when he was awarded the Elliot Silver Medal for drawing.

Despite his academic achievements, there is evidence that Eric Knight missed Yorkshire and the people of Bewerley, and there is a sense of homesick-ness in some of his artwork, and it is also reflected in the recollections of friends to whom he gave his carved wooden collie dogs. The advent of the First World War, however, put a stop to any career plans he might have nursed. Instead he travelled to Toronto and enlisted as a private to serve in Princess Patricia's Canadian Light Infantry. Again he crossed the Atlantic and saw action as a signaller in France.

The war once more brought tragedy to the Knight family. Although Eric had never been close to his two older brothers Edmund and Frederick, he was greatly saddened when he heard they had enrolled with the US Army in the Pennsylvania 110th Artillery and had both been killed in France on the same day, 30 June 1918. His mother also passed away in the same year, and Eric was left an orphan. The previous year, however, he had met and fallen in love with a Boston girl, Dorothy Noyes, and they got married, resulting in three daughters, Betty, Winifred and Jennie.

At the end of the war Eric Knight tried to resume his career as an artist in America but discovered that he was colour-blind. Although he never altogether gave up painting, he found work instead as a cartoonist and journalist with sev-eral newspapers including the *Bronx Home News*, the *Philadelphia Sun* and the *Philadelphia Public Ledger*. On the *Ledger* he was given the post of movie and drama critic, where he developed a fascination with the media that lasted for the rest of his life.

In 1932 Eric's marriage disintegrated and he was divorced. He busied himself contributing articles and short stories to a variety of popular magazines, including *Liberty* – which published his first short story, 'The Two-Fifty Hat' – *Cosmopolitan*, *Esquire* and the *Saturday Evening Post*. He also remained a reserve captain of artillery in the United States Army, a position that enabled him to travel to Europe and Central America.

Once again love entered his life when he met Jere Brylawski, a writer and story editor in Philadelphia, who was to become his helpmate and invaluable critic when he progressed from newspaper articles and short stories to novels and film scripts. In 1934 he published his first novel, *Invitation to Life*, which had an underlying autobiographical theme. Then, with the sudden closure of the *Public Ledger*, he and Jere decided to head west for Hollywood. Here Eric found work at Fox and Paramount Studios, but the frustration of project after project failing to get the green light persuaded the couple to return east. The one achievement of which he was proud was the completion of his second novel, *Song on Your Bugles* (1936), set in a poor mining area of Yorkshire and describing the adolescence of an artistic young man very much like himself.

The following year Eric and Jere Knight settled on a farm near Quakertown in Bucks County, Pennsylvania. Here they planned to grow alfalfa while Eric continued his literary career. The experiment – in a beautiful part of the state with rolling hills not unlike the area of Yorkshire where Knight had grown up – began to bear fruit almost immediately.

Once again Eric drew on his rich storehouse of childhood memories – in particular some of the tales he had heard in the Creasser household about a fabulous character called Sam Small, nicknamed the 'Flying Yorkshireman'. This man, he wrote later, 'is sometimes just an ordinary mortal and sometimes godlike, like a dream come true.' He also recalled how what would ultimately become a series of short stories had begun:

> One day I had my first bad toothache. We didn't go to a dentist; I don't think there was one for miles around. My aunt said, 'We'll rub it with a bit o' laudanum, lad – and if tha' just bides patient it'll go away.' While I bided she told me the story about Sam Small training his frightened pup – trying to make it into a real, fighting Yorkshire kind of dog. He teased it so much that in desperation it bit his nose one night, and what is more it held on. His friend, hearing the row, came in, and Sam roared for him to pry the dog loose. 'Nay, Sam,' said the friend. 'Bide it, lad, for it'll be t' makin' o' t' pup.'

Eric's first story of bluff Sam Small, 'The Flying Yorkshireman', and how he learned to fly like a bird, appeared in *Story* magazine in July 1937. It was followed by several more in the same vein, describing how the indefatigable little man coped with the two selves of his split personality and how he changed a dog into a girl and back again – all of which found a delighted audience on both sides of the Atlantic. These stories were later collected in a single volume as *Sam Small, The Flying Yorkshireman* (1957).

To those who knew Eric Knight – in particular his wife Jere – it was no surprise that Yorkshire 'tykes' should have featured in his first two novels and then the 'tall stories' about Sam Small. For the couple shared a passion for collies. One that they owned named Toots was, indeed, shortly destined to play a significant role in the creation of the most famous of all Eric Knight's Yorkshire stories.

A collie and friend on the Yorkshire Moors, painted by George Vernon Stokes in 1938

a white mongrel, may have been an influence on Eric when he came to write the chapter in his story about Lassie's meeting with the travelling potter Rowlie Palmer and his white 'tyke' Toots.

However, thoughts of a story about dogs were at first far from Eric's mind as he witnessed all over again the hardship still being endured by the families in the villages around the moors as they struggled to cope with unemployment, malnutrition and hazardous working conditions. He was also upset at the sight of men having to sell their belongings to survive – in particular their beautiful collie dogs.

Anger gripped his pen, and he poured out his feelings in an article about the inequities of the dole, 'Britain's Black Ghost', which the *Saturday Evening Post* published in its May 1938 issue. It was arguably the first essay to bring home to the American public – living as most of them were in comfort and plenty – the plight of their cousins across the Atlantic. As Jere later commented: 'Eric was a gifted proletarian writer who is sometimes forgotten because English critics think of him as an American writer and Americans think of him as an English writer.'

With the memories of the hard times in his native country fresh in his mind – not to mention the threat of war with Nazi Germany looming ever closer to Britain – he returned to the haven of his farm in Pennsylvania with ideas for more stories and books growing in his imagination. He was determined to show the English working class as people of a stubborn nature with an awareness of social injustice and yet still the possessors of remarkable artistic sensibilities. Eric would use his writing skills to try to promote reform for them all.

One of the results was a sardonic novel, *The Happy Land* (perhaps deliberately retitled for British readers *Now We Pray for Our Country*), which described the disintegration of a Yorkshire mining family under the pressures of unemployment and the dole. It was published in 1940 to critical acclaim but poor sales. Undeterred, Eric wandered the red hills around his farm with Toots at his heels, mulling over more ideas. It occurred to him that if people were going to understand the plight of the working class in England he needed to present their story in a subtler, less dark and certainly more engaging format. He would write a novelette dealing with the issues, but he would put the devotion of a Yorkshire collie at the heart of the drama because he felt this would appeal to readers of all ages.

'At the end of each day, when Eric was writing about Lassie,' Jere recalled, 'he'd always read what he'd written to his daughter, Betty, and me. And we'd sit there, with tears rolling down our faces over the sad parts, saying, "You can't *do* that!"'

'It', of course, was *Lassie Come Home*. But as Eric finished his manuscript he had no idea of the impact it would have. 'I thought it was just a neat job of bread-and-butter workmanship,' he commented later. The *Saturday Evening Post* certainly liked it enough to publish just before Christmas 1938. And within a matter of months a legend began to form around the tale and its creation, its subsequent elaboration into a novel and particularly its phenomenal appeal.

One of the earliest of these 'facts' was that Eric had been inspired to write his narrative after the disappearance one day of Toots and her equally sudden reappearance a while later. As for the name Lassie, there were lots of suggestions. One of the most popular was that collie had been called after a dog who saved a seaman's life on New Year's Day 1915 when the British battleship *Formidable* was hit by a torpedo from a German U-boat in the English Channel with the loss of more than five hundred men. The bodies of a number of these men were recovered and placed in a public house in Lyme Regis. The pub's dog, a collie, apparently began to lick the face of one 'corpse', Able Seaman John Cowan, until he suddenly started showing signs of life. Seeing this, the local doctor had Cowan

ARTHUR WARDLE.

**'Lassie Come Home', a picture by Arthur Wardle for the *Saturday Evening Post***

rushed to the nearest hospital where he eventually recovered. According to a local tradition the dog's name was Lassie – and *she* was Eric Knight's inspiration. The author himself remained silent on this point, although he did acknowledge his debt to Toots by using her name for the travelling potter's scruffy mongrel.

The original novelette differs in several respects from Eric's full-length book, and this probably accounts for some of the misapprehensions that have grown up around the story. For example, the shorter version actually begins from Lassie's point of view with a moving scene that sets the entire mood of the tale:

> The dog had met the boy by the school gate for five years. Now she couldn't understand that times were changed and she wasn't supposed to be there any more. But the boy knew. So when he opened the door of the cottage, he spoke before he entered. 'Mother,' he said, 'Lassie's come home again.'

The 'black, white and gold collie', the story tells us, has been sold to the Duke of Rudling (the first of many names derived from the West Riding setting of the story) in order to save the Carraclough family (elements of Eric's uncle and aunt here) from poverty after the father, Sam, is laid off after seventeen backbreaking years in the local mines. His son Joe – perhaps the author himself – is the twelve-year-old boy so delighted at the first of what will prove to be several 'homecomings' by the faithful collie.

In this original version the setting of Greenhall Bridge is more obviously Bewerley, although the name itself is a variation on Pateley Bridge. There are also mines in the district of the kind referred to by Eric Knight but not *coal* mines. Lead-mining is the preserve of this part of Yorkshire, although his descriptions of the Clarabelle and Wellington pits match the once-thriving Cockhill and Providence mines that the author must have passed a hundred times on his youthful walks.

The collie-breeding Duke of Rudling's local estate, 'a mile from the village', is a thinly disguised Bewerley Old Hall with its cottages and high-walled, old-world gardens. The Duke's Scottish estate is firmly located on the far north coast facing the Shetland Islands. For reasons best known to himself, Eric Knight changed the name of the duke's sympathetic granddaughter from Philippa in the *Saturday Evening Post* to Priscilla in the book. Lassie is also deliberately *sent* to Scotland to prevent her running away, which is precisely what she does and defies all the odds to get back to Yorkshire in an epic journey that almost kills her. It is a trek that is so poignantly told that it can hardly fail to leave any reader unmoved:

> A thousand miles of tor and brae, of shire and moor, of path and road and plowland, of river and stream and burn and brook and beck, of snow and rain and fog and sun, is a long way, even for a human being. But it would seem too far – much, much too far – for any dog to travel blindly and win through.

But of course Lassie *does* win through and in a wholly satisfactory conclusion is able to remain with the family, while Sam Carraclough is hired by the Duke to be his dog handler. This is a finale common to both versions – although the original novella ends on a more dramatic note with Rudling giving instructions to the

Carracloughs to 'get rid of that misshapen mongrel'. Young Joe is happy to agree:

> 'In a day or so we'll have her fixed up and coped up so's ye'd never, never recognize her,' said Joe.
>      'I don't doubt,' the Duke puffed as he went to his car, 'ye could do exactly that.'

Eric Knight may well have regarded his story as 'bread-and-butter workmanship', but John C. Winston, head of a publishing company in Philadelphia, read it in the *Saturday Evening Post* and saw far greater potential. He contacted the author and commissioned him to turn it into a full-length novel. When Eric delivered the manuscript a year later – significantly dedicated to Dr Harry Jarrett, who had played an important role in collie-breeding in America – he also submitted a series of his own illustrations. However, Winston declined the offer as he was already set on an illustrator named Marguerite Kirmse who had become very popular in America for her drawings and prints of dogs. Considering the origins of the story, she was a very suitable choice.

Like Eric Knight, Marguerite Kirmse had been born in England in 1885, in the fashionable south-coast seaside resort of Bournemouth. She had studied art and music in London and supported herself at first by playing the harp. However, Marguerite got greater satisfaction from drawing animals and, after honing her skills sketching animal anatomy at the London Zoo, moved to New York in the 1920s. Here, under the tutelage of Frank Calderon, she began to specialize in drawing dogs of all breeds, shapes and sizes. Despite the Depression that hit the USA, Marguerite Kirmse found herself in demand with the public for prints – especially of Scottie dogs – and by publishers to illustrate their books. She was a natural choice for *Lassie Come Home* and created the first images of Lassie which have been a source of inspiration to artists and illustrators ever since. The book remains the most famous of all those she illustrated.

Kirmse provided thirty-six illustrations for *Lassie Come Home*, which went through an astonishing eighteen printings in America during the two years following publication. Eventually Eric's book was translated into twenty-five languages,

with Marguerite's illustrations being reprinted in many of them. Thanks to her success as an illustrator and etcher, she was able to buy a farm in Connecticut where she bred terriers and field dogs until her death in 1954.

Success for Eric was, however, still some way off when he finished work on

**Portrait of Lassie by
Marguerite Kirmse for the
cover of the first edition
of *Lassie Come Home*,
published in March 1940**

*Lassie Come Home.* In 1940 he spent a year running a course in 'Writing Fiction' at the University of Iowa in Iowa City, where his passion for the written word and the social concerns he aired in his classes and lectures made him popular with his pupils. One of these recalled years later that his 'Knightian enthusiasm was a byword in student circles'.

By now the Second World War had enveloped Britain, and Eric volunteered his services to the British Ministry of Information. He also wrote a new novel, *This Above All* (1941), a tragic love story set during the Battle of Britain that explored the ambivalence and bitterness of its working-class hero, a soldier, towards English society. It was immediately acclaimed as 'the first great novel to come out of the Second World War', sold over 35,000 copies in Britain alone and the following year was filmed with Tyrone Power and Joan Fontaine.

The demands of the war frequently separated Eric from Toots, with pre-dictable results, as Jere has recalled: 'When he was in Washington, on military duty, she used to sit at the front gate of our farm in Bucks County and watch for him.' Eric also felt the pangs of separation, writing in a letter to a friend, 'My old lady Toots is getting a bit grey, more feeble. I sorrow about her and she sorrows for us away in the war. She's a big chunk of my life and history, with all the thousands of miles she's travelled with us, and she can't understand these war-time absences.'

In October 1941 master and dog were parted again when Eric crossed the Atlantic to begin work on the Ministry of Information's film *World of Plenty*. While there he also lectured and delivered radio talks about America to British listeners. The following year, with the USA now in the war, Eric returned to America and was commissioned as a captain in the Special Services Division. He helped in compiling military guidebooks about England and Egypt and worked on several war-film projects with the Hollywood director Frank Capra. Foremost among these was the Army documentary series 'Why We Fight', the first of which, *Prelude to War*, won an Oscar for best documentary in 1942. Capra never forgot his association with Eric and wrote affectionately about him in his autobiography *Frank Capra: The Name Above the Title* (1971): 'Eric Knight was a red-moustached American captain with a British accent; a Yorkshireman whose unruly shock of red hair seemed as full of mischief as his sharp, ferret-like eyes. He had all the talents that could be compressed into a single writer: wit, compassion, sensitiveness, an intriguing style; and a great, great love for human beings.'

Among all these duties Eric found time to sign the films rights for *Lassie Come Home* to MGM for $10,000. He was invited to help in selecting the collie for the lead role and expressed his delight at the final choice of Pal. He was also pleased with the casting of a young English actor, Roddy McDowell, to play Joe and an extremely pretty but as yet unknown actress named Elizabeth Taylor as Priscilla. For all three the picture would prove a passport to stardom. After a visit to the set in Hollywood during the early days of shooting in the summer of 1942, Eric commented: 'The dog is the most magnificent collie I've ever seen – in conformation, colour and brilliant sense. Oh, gladly do I call him a movie star. I coveted him more than I ever did [Joan] Fontaine, [Dorothy] Lamour and

'Oh, gladly do I call him a movie star' – Eric Knight on his first meeting with Pal in Hollywood

all the other pretty stars. (They couldn't get a bitch for the part that looked right, so he's a female impersonator – and thank God he's got a long coat that covers his manhood!) Anyhow, I've been promised a son of his for the farm.'

Although there was no hint of sadness in this last remark, Eric knew that his own Toots was failing in health back in Bucks County. (She was later buried there on the farm.) He could also have had no inkling that he would not live long enough to enjoy the remarkable success of *Lassie Come Home*.

In January 1943 Captain Eric Knight was promoted to the rank of major and ordered to fly to Cairo for what was euphemistically described as 'temporary duty'. On the ill-omened date of 13 January he was flying on a TWA C-54 transport plane under contract to the Air Transport Command when the aircraft crashed in a jungle some thirty miles from Paramaribo in Dutch Guiana (now Suriname), killing him and all the other thirty-four people on board. He was just forty-five years old. The accident was the worst air disaster in the Western Hemisphere to that date and immediately prompted a conspiracy theory that has remained unsettled to this day.

It was suggested that the aircraft was actually on the way to a top-secret conference in Casablanca – a claim made more probable by the presence on board of two FBI agents and a State Department official. There were also rumours of a bomb, which had already caused the pilot, Captain Benjamin Dally, to land once at Trinidad to search the plane. Although an implement containing an IFF (Identification Friend or Foe) device was found in the hatch, there were no signs of any explosives. After the crash, however, security was increased at all American air bases around the world and there was a clampdown on the release of any more information.

An investigation of the crash site under the auspices of US Major General Harold George is believed to have located a number of secret coded documents intended for the British General Sir Harold Alexander as well as a large amount of money, possibly destined for the buying of support and information for the Allied cause. Some pointers to the nature of the mission are also to be found among Eric's papers held at Yale. These include the curious contents of a musette bag, a document, *Hints on Pronouncing Arabic*, and a chart of 'Special Services Operations'.

The apparent importance and secrecy surrounding the mission was, however, of little comfort to Jere Knight or her husband's four daughters. Even the posthumous award of the US Legion of Merit to Eric and his burial in the Jefferson Barracks National Cemetery in St Louis, Missouri, was not enough to assuage the grief felt by the family, not forgetting the ever-growing band of admirers of *Lassie Come Home* on both sides of the Atlantic. Today Eric's granddaughter, Betsy Mewborn Cowan, is pursuing a campaign via the internet on behalf of all the thirty-five victims to discover the real cause of the crash; she can be contacted by anyone possessing information at olgaswen@aol.com.

The name of Eric Knight has, of course, lived on through the editions of his book, the films, television series and radio broadcasts featuring his immortal collie. They provide a tribute to the Yorkshire lad who turned the mutual love of a boy and his dog into an enduring masterpiece. It was fitting that when the very first film of *Lassie Come Home* opened in America a few months after his death it should feature an opening frame that read simply: *Dedicated to the Memory of Eric Knight.*

Canine trainer Rudd Weatherwax with Pal, the original Lassie

# CHAPTER SIX

# A Star Is Born

A STRANGE TWIST OF fate in the summer of 1942 turned an unlikely two-year-old collie named Pal into Lassie, the most famous screen dog of the twentieth century. The dog was actually smaller than a standard collie, lacked the breed's long, thin nose and had a narrow white blaze that turned into an oval on his forehead – all features disliked by top breeders. Yet Pal, whose faults also included disobedience and a habit of chasing motor cycles whenever he saw them, was undeniably a highly intelligent, strikingly beautiful and very photogenic animal.

The train of events that brought Pal to the MGM Studios in Hollywood while pre-production was under way that summer for the screen version of *Lassie Come Home* had begun several months earlier when he was taken by his exasperated original owner to a training school in the city run by Frank and Rudd (short for Ruddell) Weatherwax. The brothers were from a family that had a long association with animals, and they would ultimately play a leading part in training some of the best-known dogs for the movies. They were the sons of a larger-than-life character, Walter 'Smiley' Weatherwax, who had ridden with Buffalo Bill's Wild

# LASSIE

West Show, had to flee Texas to avoid a murder charge after avenging the death of his partner killed in a dispute over the ownership of two horses and moved to Los Angeles in 1911 in the hope of finding work in the burgeoning film business.

It was shortly after settling in the town with their father that Frank and Rudd Weatherwax acquired their first puppies and discovered they had a natural aptitude for teaching the dogs tricks such as retrieving money from the floor or fetching apples from a stall as far as two streets away. Father and sons all got work as extras in a number of westerns, with the boys often taking their dogs along to the studios and getting them to perform stunts in the hope of obtaining work.

In 1925 the brothers were spotted with their versatile dogs outside one studio gate by an established trainer, Henry East, who offered them work. In the years that followed they helped to provide dogs for a variety of films, including Asta, a wire-haired terrier who appeared in the *Thin Man* movies staring William Powell and Myrna Loy, and the lovable mongrel Daisy who co-starred in the *Blondie* films with Penny Singleton. In the late 1930s Frank and Rudd opened the Studio Dog Training School, which became increasingly well known. Then in 1942 they were presented with the collie that would make them famous and change the history of dogs on the screen for ever.

Although his owner told Frank Rudd all about Pal's bad habits, Frank agreed to try to train the collie. Several days later, according to June Johns of *Picture Post* magazine writing in April 1947, the owner called the kennels to say he 'could not afford the fees after all' and suggested the Weatherwax brothers keep his unruly dog. They knew they faced a real challenge but sensed that the alert and handsome dog might have a future in films if he was methodically trained.

As the two trainers hoped, the collie proved a quick learner, and when MGM put out a casting call for *Lassie Come Home* Pal was taken to the studios. Hundreds of other hopeful pets also turned up. Director Fred Wilcox was impressed by Pal's ability but not his appearance – his coat had apparently been damaged while he was undergoing preliminary training with Rudd on a ranch in the California hills – and he was rejected without even a screen test.

June Johns picks up the story: 'Convinced that his dog *could* pay the role, Rudd began an intensive training course. He taught the dog to crawl, attack, open doors and even to yawn. He brushed and combed him twice a day and gave him regular sulphur baths to get his coat in condition. All the while, the search for a Lassie continued from one end of the continent to the other.'

When Rudd Weatherwax took Pal back to MGM again he was frustrated to discover that in the interim a show collie had been hired and was now undergoing her own training for the part. However, Pal was offered the role of stand-in and Rudd decided to accept – a decision he would never have cause to regret.

Fate soon intervened again when the Sacramento river in northern California suddenly flooded. The script of *Lassie Come Home* demanded a scene with the runaway collie crossing a swollen river, and Fred Wilcox decided to seize the opportunity. Although only Technicolor cameras were available for what was planned to be a black-and-white picture, he decided to go ahead with a shoot at the location. However, it was immediately apparent that the show collie was not yet ready to duplicate the necessary actions: emerging slowly from the river and falling on the bank, too exhausted even to shake herself.

So Pal and Rudd Weatherwax were given the opportunity instead. The one-time rebellious dog plunged into the racing water, hauled himself from the flow with his head hung low as if it was almost too heavy to carry and fell on to the grass bank, seemingly on the verge of collapse. A star had been born, as June Johns later explained: 'The very faults in his coat that had made Pal unfit for shows made him photogenic. When the footage was shown to the head of MGM, Louis B. Mayer, he sat silent for a moment and then remarked, "Pal entered the water, but Lassie came out of it." He was rechristened on the spot and began his reign as the greatest star in the dog world.'

**Pal becomes a star when he emerges from the Sacramento River while filming *Lassie Come Home***

# A STAR IS BORN

The *Picture Post* article also provided readers with an insight into the life that the 'great star' enjoyed after *Lassie Come Home* was released to the world's cinemas. Apart from a five-year contract at a salary of $50,000 a year, Pal aka Lassie was soon receiving five hundred fan letters a week and getting very special treatment. His diet was made up of two pounds of prime meat a day, a thorough daily grooming and a bath once a month.

'Not for him the ordinary dog-house,' June Johns wrote of Pal's life while making the next three films in the series.

He had a special kennel designed and built for him and when he went on location in the mountains, the kennel went, too, traveling thousands of miles before it dropped to pieces. Now he has a regular star's dressing room with a couch where he rests between shots. A Prevention of Cruelty to Animals representative spends all his working hours on the set seeing that the dog is not overworked.

But there is no fear of that. As soon as Lassie gets tired, as he does with remarkable punctuality after seven hours' work, he stops being an actor and behaves like any ordinary dog. He refuses to come when called, wags his tail when he should groan as though in pain, and does all he can to wreck the scene. Cameramen and directors have learned that no amount of persuasion will make him work overtime. In any case, they must take the greatest care that he doesn't make himself ill or stale with work, for the livelihoods of nearly a thousand men and women depend on Lassie when a film is being made.

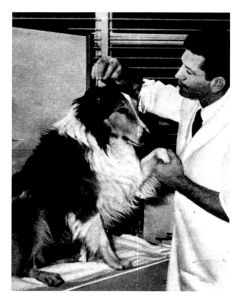

**Lassie gets her daily grooming from MGM make-up artist Jack Young**

The writer explained that the collie worked about six months of the year and for the rest of the time lived a normal though rather pampered life as Rudd Weatherwax's pet.

He sleeps at the foot of Rudd's bed, much to the disgust of Mrs Weatherwax who gets cramp in her feet with Lassie's weight! Apart from the film tricks, such as rolling over and pawing the ground, pretending he is in pain, Lassie has been taught some useful everyday tricks. For instance, when Rudd's two youngsters stray from the back garden and roam into the fields, Rudd saves his own legs and lungs by sending Lassie after them. The dog races away and, having located the children, runs around them barking, trying to head them home as a sheepdog might. Sometimes the children don't want to go home and refuse to be led, in which case Lassie resorts to force. He takes the children, one at a time, by the wrist, and gently, but firmly, pulls them home. Never once has he scratched them.

Rudd Weatherwax also told June Johns some of his training secrets. At the heart of his work, he said, was a belief that there was no point in even trying with a dog that would not chase a ball or any other moving object. It was also vital to teach the animal to understand a tone of voice rather than special commands. He did not believe in punishing a dog but rewarding him when he obeyed a command. It was important to realize that the training of an animal could be slow, and a dog should never be worn down so that he no longer enjoyed obeying his instructor.

At the start of training, Rudd said, the dog should have about ten minutes a day with a ball. It should be thrown and followed by a command in one or two words to 'fetch it'. It might take several days for the dog to understand the command, but it was important not to lose patience or beat the animal. When the ball *was* retrieved, the dog should be rewarded – although not every time, he said. The length of every lesson should be gradually increased, too. Tricks could be introduced such as placing a biscuit on the ground in front of the dog and then putting him 'on trust' not to eat it until he has been given permission.

Rudd believed that training should begin by the time a dog was about six months old, and the owner must be prepared to continue for years if necessary. He also said it was important that the lessons were carried out in private without any audience as all dogs concentrated better without any distractions. According to June Johns, Lassie recognized only Rudd Weatherwax's voice, and on one occasion when he was ill the whole production was held up. His brother Frank was then recruited as a 'reserve voice' to cover for any future eventualities. The *Picture Post* article concluded: 'Rudd has set up a trust fund which assures the dog

**Years of training are required for a stunt like this with Lassie leaping from a blazing house in *The Hills of Home* (1949)**

life-long care no matter what happens to the Weatherwaxes or his screen career. Yet in his leisure, Lassie still loves to ruin his fur on the underbrush and, confesses Rudd, despite all the training, he still chases motor cycles!'

In fact the trust fund was not required as Rudd Weatherwax prospered in his role and lived until 1985. On his death, his son Bob – one of the children rounded up all those years previously from the garden by the original Lassie – took over the breeding and training of each generation of collie puppies to fill the star role in movies and on television. It was a seamless transition for Bob Weatherwax, who had actually been born one year to the very day after the original Pal. Bob's subsequent career has landed him a number of major film credits as animal trainer apart from the Lassie films, including John Carpenter's Arctic horror story *The Thing*

(1982) and the Steven Spielberg science-fiction thriller *Back to the Future* (1985).

For the record, eight generations of the Weatherwax collies have appeared on screen since that original star was born. They are as follows:

| Stage name | Call name | Trainer |
|---|---|---|
| Lassie 1 | Pal | Rudd Weatherwax |
| Lassie 2 | Lassie Jr (son of Pal) | Rudd Weatherwax |
| Lassie 3 | Baby (son of Lassie Jr) | Rudd Weatherwax |
| Lassie 4 | Mire | Rudd Weatherwax |
| Lassie 5 | Hey Hey | Rudd Weatherwax |
| Lassie 6 | Boy (son of Hey Hey) | Rudd Weatherwax |
| Lassie 7 | The Old Man | Rudd Weatherwax |
| Lassie 8 | Howard | Bob Weatherwax |

The first collie movie star Madeleine and her owner,
the French actress Huguette Duflos, photographed in 1936

# CHAPTER SEVEN

# Greer Garson in Furs

THERE IS ANOTHER, perhaps understandable, belief that Lassie was the first rough collie 'star' in films. In fact, some five years before the release of *Lassie Come Home* a striking tricolour French collie named Madeleine appeared twice on the screen in 1938 with her actress owner Huguette Duflos in *Le Train pour Venise* (*The Train for Venice*) and *Visages de femmes* (*Faces of Women*). In both pictures the well-trained and beautifully prepared dog gave scene-stealing performances that resulted in a demand for collie puppies in France.

Huguette, a striking blonde with beguiling eyes and a slim figure, had played a number of leading roles in French films after reigning for a decade as 'the ornament of the French stage' at La Comédie Française from 1915 to 1927. He first film role was in the 1916 silent, *Madeleine*, co-starring Jean Kemm, and she later chose the title for the name of her first collie, purchased in 1934. In subsequent pictures Huguette made something of a speciality of playing mature *femmes fatales* in films such as *The Unknown Woman* (1917), *The Trap of Love* (1920) and *The Man with the Hispano* (1926). Major stardom came in the great opera movie

*Der Rosenkavalier* (1926), directed by Robert Weine, followed by *The Mystery of the Yellow Room* (1931) based on the best-selling crime novel by Gaston Leroux, author of *The Phantom of the Opera* (1925). In this she played Mlle Strangerson, a scientist's daughter targeted for murder by an unknown assailant who is finally unmasked by the detective Joseph Rouletabille (Roland Toutain).

The success of these pictures thrust Huguette Duflos into the heart of Paris society, and she became a familiar figure during the 1930s at the leading restaurants and nightclubs, often with Madeleine by her side. The glamorous pair proved irresistible to photographers, and pictures of them appeared in numerous newspapers and magazines. Such was the appeal of the collie that when director André Berthomieu cast Huguette in *Le Train pour Venise* in 1938 he decided that the collie would make an ideal companion for her in the role of a fashionable Parisian wife Caroline Ancelot whose husband discovers she is using walks with the dog as an excuse for meetings with her penniless lover. Later the same year Madeleine appeared in several scenes in *Visages de femmes* in which her owner is a member of a 'fast set' whose voluptuous lifestyle is shattered when one of the women becomes pregnant as a result of a love affair with a raffish tennis player.

Huguette Duflos made her last film, *Le Capitaine*, in 1945 and retired to the South of France where she kept a number of collies until her death in 1982. Madeleine's progeny are still to be found in Paris and St Tropez where another famous French star, Brigitte Bardot, owned a rough collie among the dogs at her beach bungalow La Madrague on the Baie des Caroubiers.

One of Bardot's great rivals as a sex symbol, Elizabeth Taylor, actually owed her break into films to a collie in the first Lassie movie, *Lassie Come Home*, made in 1942. Faithfully scripted from Eric Knight's novel by Hugo Butler, it retained much of the plot and a considerable amount of the dialogue. The success of the young actress after the picture is all the more remarkable because, as she later told Donald Spoto for his biography *Elizabeth Taylor* (1995), 'I never wanted a career – it was forced on me.' In fact it was her ambitious mother, Sara, who had great plans for her, made her sing and dance before friends and visitors and then in April 1941 engineered a contract for her with Universal Pictures at a weekly salary of $100 when she was just nine years old.

Initially Universal could find nothing suitable for the little girl until – according to a Hollywood tradition – Elizabeth's father had a chance meeting in the autumn of 1942 with MGM producer Samuel Marx, who was having difficulty finding 'a little girl with an English accent for a small role in *Lassie Come Home*'. Francis Taylor suggested his daughter, and the offer was eagerly accepted. In fact, as Donald Spoto discovered, when Sara Taylor heard about Marx's quandary she actually urged her husband to badger the producer for a part for their daughter.

'*Lassie Come Home* was already in production,' Spoto has written, 'but the girl contracted for the small supporting role was too tall to play opposite 14-year-old Roddy McDowall, the leading player with whom she would have several scenes. In 1942 such a disparity in height was an untenable cinematic situation. Sara proposed her daughter as a substitute and the rest is history.'

Elizabeth Taylor's ability to speak perfectly clipped English made her ideally

**Roddy McDowall reads a copy of *Lassie Come Home* with his co-star on the set of the first movie in the series (1943)**

suited to play opposite McDowall, who had been a leading child actor in his native London and came to Hollywood to work with Twentieth Century Fox, which – like Universal with his co-star – had nothing suitable and loaned him out to MGM for this film. Under the astute direction of Fred Wilcox, McDowall playing Joe Carraclough and Elizabeth the Duke of Rudling's granddaughter Priscilla gave endearing performances, but it was the 'radiant Pal, carefully lit and edited to imitate the feelings of a method actor' (Spoto), who was the star. Even the other adult actors, Donald Crisp (Sam Carraclough), Elsa Lanchester (Mrs Carraclough) and Nigel Bruce (the Duke of Rudling), had to play second fiddle to Rudd Weatherwax's dog.

The film was a box-office success on both sides of the Atlantic – particularly in France, where *Fidèle Lassie* excited fresh interest in collies in the wake of the Huguette Duflos movies – and a *Variety* reviewer was so moved by the personal appeal of the collie's performance that he compared the dog to another of

MGM's leading ladies, calling him 'Greer Garson in Furs'. Predictably, the film company was soon hard at work on a follow-up, *Son of Lassie* (1944). In this sequel, written by Jeanne Bartlett, the time has moved forward to the Second World War with Joe Carraclough, now an adult, in the RAF and about to be followed at every step of his mission by Lassie's son Laddie – Pal now doubling as 'her' own son. The collie comes to Joe's assistance after he has been shot down behind enemy lines in Norway by tracking him for over forty miles.

Directed by Sylvan Simon, *Son of Lassie* saw the return of Donald Crisp and Nigel Bruce, with a pretty young actress, June Lockhart (who would later star in the *Lassie* TV series), replacing Elizabeth Taylor as the grown-up Priscilla and Peter Lawford – of 'Rat Pack' fame – getting his first starring role as Joe. It was an opportunity Lawford relished but provided more hardships than pleasures during the location shoot around Patricia Bay near Vancouver, British Columbia, as he later rather tartly told his biographer James Spada in *Peter Lawford* (1998): 'You want to know how we did those scenes of affection between man and dog? I had raw meat stuck under my arms and under my shirt and rubbed on my face and stuck up my clyde and that animal was eating me alive! What you saw on screen, what you thought was the true love of a dog for his master, wasn't that at all. No, it was sheer animal hunger.'

Peter was not amused that Pal had his own dressing-room – 'he was checked into a two-bedroom suite, accompanied by a whole retinue, sort of like a small Frank Sinatra unit' – nor that the collie had been insured for a million dollars while doing a number of scenes in the treacherous waters of the Columbia River

# LASSIE

**Peter Lawford, who had problems working with his co-star on the second movie, *Son of Lassie* (1945)**

rapids. 'I had the suspicion that if I was insured at all, it was for a substantially smaller amount,' he said.

Despite these problems, *Son of Lassie* was another success, earned Lawford excellent notices and put him on the road to stardom. Soon MGM had Fred Wilcox busy on a third picture in which the maturing Elizabeth Taylor – fresh from her success in the romantic equine film *National Velvet* – was to star again with Pal. *Hold High the Torch*, scripted by Lionel Houser, recounted the exploits of a collie named Bill who is reared by young Kathie Merrick (Taylor) and then accidentally lost and trained to be a war dog with a K9 Corps unit (geddit?) lead by Sergeant Smitty (Tom Drake).

The evidence in the MGM archives suggests that the company did not decide until shooting was nearly over that the picture should take full advantage of the two stars' successful first collaboration in *Lassie Come Home*. By the time the film was released in the summer of 1946 it had been retitled *The Courage of Lassie*. Once again Rudd Weatherwax's collie stole most of the accolades and proved especially adept at mimicking mental and physical exhaustion and even briefly playing a mad-dog chicken killer.

Elizabeth Taylor, unlike Peter Lawford, liked working with Pal and undertook considerable publicity for the launch of *The Courage of Lassie*. The weekly magazine *Life* ran a story, 'Elizabeth Taylor Loves Animals and Out-of-doors', in its issue of 26 February 1946 which claimed that her quiet, affectionate personality had a 'hypnotic effect on dogs and horses'. Of her co-star, Taylor said, 'I was thrilled to be working with Lassie. She was already a big star.'

None the less, the changes that were made during the shooting of the third picture are probably one of the reasons why the Lassie series began to suffer a decline in popularity. Indeed, when the green light was given for a fourth picture in 1948, her name was dropped from the title in what was apparently an attempt to catch a more diverse audience. *Hills of Home* was written by William Ludwig based on the Scottish author Ian Maclaren's sketches *Doctor of the Old School*, which had previously been filmed in 1923 without, of course, Lassie. The story, with Fred Wilcox again as director, returned to Eric Knight's original Scottish territory and the struggles of a GP, William MacLure (Edmund Gwenn), to bring

A rare poster for the third film in the series, *Courage of Lassie* (1946)

modern medicine to his patients. Along the way he adopts a water-shy Lassie and slowly cures the dog of her phobia until, in a fitting climax, she is able to dive into a raging river and save him from drowning.

The rescue episode, and another scene about the practical use of ether in which Lassie was cleverly involved, made the film popular with long-time admirers of the series who were apparently able to forgive the script referring to the dog as 'Girl' and 'Lass'. Later, in fact, the film would be re-released as *Master of Lassie*. Edmund Gwenn – a Welsh-born character actor who had won an Oscar the previous year as Santa Claus in *Miracle on 34th Street* – gave a moving performance alongside Pal. The critics also singled out Donald Crisp, returning to the series as a dour Scot, Drumsheugh, and a young actress, Janet Leigh, playing a pretty village girl, Margit Mitchell, a decade ahead of her performance in Alfred Hitchcock's terrifying thriller *Psycho* (1960).

The story on which the fifth movie in the series was based, *The Sun Comes Up*, had a curiously similar gestation to *Lassie Come Home*. In December 1936 the American writer Marjorie Kinnan Rawlings had written a poignant short tale, 'A Mother in Mannville', about the tribulations of an orphan, Jerry, which had been published in the *Saturday Evening Post*. A decade later, after the huge success of her novel *The Yearling*, about a boy and his pet deer, Rawlings was asked to turn her short story into a novel and produced *Mountain Prelude* (1947), in which a bitter pianist-composer, Helen Jackson, who has lost her only son recovers by mothering Jerry and his inseparable canine friend. MGM saw an opportunity to utilize the success of *The Yearling* by adapting this story for the screen and giving a starring role to the Broadway singer-actress Jeanette MacDonald, famous for her duets with Nelson Eddy. It would also provide another outing for their canine star in a number of scene-stealing tricks.

*The Sun Comes Up* (1949), scripted by Margaret Fitts and William Ludwig and directed by Richard Thorpe, contained some touching moments between MacDonald and her youthful co-star Claude Jarman Jr – who had previously starred in the movie version of *The Yearling* – as well as a dramatic rescue scene with Lassie pulling her master from a burning loft. However, MGM's decision not to include the dog's name in the title is an indication of their declining commitment to the series, although the French showed greater faith by releasing the picture as *Lassie, perdue et gagnée* (*Lassie Lost and Found*). The film is also of interest in movie history for having provided the début for a twenty-year-old musical arranger destined for great things named André Previn.

Purists were not amused, though, when the sixth picture, *Challenge to Lassie*, was put into production later the same year. The film, directed again by Richard Thorpe, was an unabashed adaptation of the famous Scottish legend *Greyfriars Bobby*, about a Skye terrier who had sat on guard for twelve years at his master's graveside in Edinburgh. Using the definitive book by Eleanor Atkinson, scriptwriter William Ludwig substituted Lassie for the terrier and had her bringing to justice a gang of young toughs who set about her master Jock Gray (Donald Crisp), killing him as he brings his flock of sheep to market. A young Geraldine Brooks played Lassie's saviour who defies the local officials too busy trying to put down the resolute collie to notice her indications as to the identities of the killers.

Singer-actress Jeanette MacDonald and Claude Jarman Jr discuss Lassie's future in *The Sun Comes Up* (1949)

Interestingly, Donald Crisp would appear in a more faithful version of *Greyfriars Bobby* made in 1963 by Walt Disney, playing the graveyard keeper.

Despite an intensive publicity and merchandising campaign, *Challenge to Lassie* did not win a new generation of movie fans for the canine hero. Indeed, MGM only made one more picture before relinquishing their rights to the series. *The Painted Hills* (1951), scripted by True Boardman and directed by Harold F. Kress, has been described as 'the most dreadful Lassie movie ever made', and it is difficult to dispute this verdict.

Once again the picture is based on a novel, *Shep of the Painted Hills* by Alexander Hull, in which a prospector, Jonathan Harvey (Paul Kelly), strikes gold after years of backbreaking work but is denied success by his greedy partner. Only

*Challenge To Lassie* (1949), which incorporated another famous
canine Scottish legend, Greyfriars Bobby, into the storyline

Harvey's clever collie, Shep, aka Lassie, is witness to the fatal double-cross. But with the aid of young Tommy Blake (Gary Gray), and surviving several attempts to shoot and poison him, Shep finally sees justice served. The bleak plot, uninspired dialogue and a particularly vicious scene in which the implacable, growling canine star faced the killer certainly did not endear *The Painted Hills* to younger audiences. Even two attempts at retitling the picture as *Lassie's Adventures in the Gold Rush* and *Lassie's Christmas Adventure* could not disguise the poor quality, and MGM wrote *finis* to the series that had generated seven films in under a decade.

It would be almost a quarter of a century before Lassie returned to the cinema. In the meantime, however, Eric Knight's rough collie would become a favourite in two other mediums – radio and television. The impact of the broadcast word and of small-screen serials would ensure that the legend of the extraordinary dog continued to evolve and reach an even wider audience.

Tommy Rettig, first star of the long-running *Lassie* television series, with Lassie – the son of Pal and only dog of that name to play the role

# CHAPTER EIGHT

# The World's Most Famous Dog

O N SUNDAY 12 September 1954 a lone collie appeared on television screens across America first drinking water on the shore of a lake and then responding to the call of her name. It was a modest beginning to a series that would run for over 675 episodes and earn its canine star the accolade of 'the world's most famous dog'. The black-and-white programme marked the final transition of Lassie from Eric Knight's short story to a novel, then the cinema and finally into a thirty-minute weekly CBS production that has since been seen all over the world.

No longer, though, was Lassie running across the Yorkshire moors or the hills of Scotland; now her home was farmland in the Midwest of America. Here she lived with young Jeff Miller, his widowed mother Ellen and grandfather. Against the background of this rural idyll the collie was the hero in a seemingly endless series of stories ranging from simple farmyard problems to dramatic rescues in which the super-intelligent dog invariably intervened to prevent disaster. It was a reworking of Eric Knight's simple formula of a boy and his dog united by love and bravery, destined to earn *Lassie* two Emmy Awards as Best Children's Series in

1955 and 1956 and become the longest-running children's series on American television.

The legends that have attached themselves to the programme began with the very first episode, 'Inheritance'. In a neat volte-face Lassie was seen as reluctant to leave her master, Homer Carey, when the old man was insistent on giving her to young Jeff. It was a moving story that many viewers claim to remember because of the unforgettable 'whistling theme' that introduced the show. In fact this unique tune, composed by Les Baxter and 'whistled' by Muzzy Marcellino, was not actually introduced into the series for another three years. The original theme song was 'Secret of the Silent Hills', written in 1940 by William Lava, and it was not replaced by its famous successor until 1957.

It is also a fact that the TV programme was not the first Lassie series broadcast in the USA. That distinction belongs to the ABC radio network, which launched a fifteen-minute weekly show, *Lassie*, in the autumn of 1947 in the wake of the successful movie *Courage of Lassie*. The programme was sponsored by Red Heart dog food and featured Charles Lyon as the announcer. The radio show also had its own special refrain, 'Comin' Through the Rye', based on the old folk tune by Robbie Burns. The main scriptwriter was the radio veteran Hobe Donovan, with Marvin Miller and Betty Arnold voicing most of the human characters. Another misconception among listeners is that Lassie herself was heard on the air throughout the show's three-year run. Although it is certainly true that Rudd Weatherwax's Pal *did* provide a number of pre-recorded barks and growls, all the other dog sounds were created by Earl Keen, a well-known animal imitator.

When the *Lassie* television series was launched seven years later in 1954 under the sponsorship of Campbell's Soup, the original film collie, Pal, appeared in just two episodes before being replaced by his son, Lassie Jr – the only one of the line to actually bear the name. He would remain as the show's star for six years before one of his progeny filled the role. The part of Lassie's master was played by a young actor named Tommy Rettig who came to the part fresh from working with Marilyn Monroe in *River of No Return* with no idea that he was about to become co-star to another icon.

Rettig, who had been born in Jackson Heights, New York, in December 1941, had started his acting career at the age of six appearing on stage with Mary Martin in *Annie Get Your Gun*. By 1954 he had a string of credits to his name – apart from Monroe he also worked that year with Peter Ustinov and Jean Simmons in a historical epic *The Egyptian* – and settled into the part of the farm boy Jeff with practised ease. Some years later he told reporter Brendan Bourne of the *Daily Mail*: 'I got on very well with Lassie. Sometimes I even took him home, but that had to stop when Lassie got confused about whether to obey me or Rudd Weatherwax. After that I used to spend a lot of weekends with him and his son, Bob, who was the same age as me.'

Tommy also got on well with his human co-stars, Jan Clayton, playing his mother, and George Cleveland as Gramps. Jeff had a young friend on many of his exploits, Sylvester 'Porky' Brockway (Donald Keeler), although he could sometimes prove to be as much of a hindrance in a crisis as Lassie was an asset. Rettig's screen character became a fashion leader among teenagers when the black (later red) Chuck Taylor sneakers he wore were every boy's 'must have'.

Three successful years later, however, Tommy was growing too old for the role, and in the spring of 1957 a runaway orphan, Timmy, played by seven-year-old Jon Provost, was introduced to the series and soon became an integral part of the Miller household. A suitable exit for the three originals was found that autumn with the death of Gramps, leaving Jeff and his mother unable to run the farm on their own. The property was sold to a childless couple, Paul and Ruth Martin (Jon Shepodd and Cloris Leachman), who decided to adopt Timmy and keep the ever-faithful Lassie. The formula continued to appeal to viewers, and there was no discernable difference in these figures when, a year later, June Lockhart and Hugh Reilly took over the roles of the Martins. They remained with the show for six years, becoming the best known of all the adults to appear in *Lassie*.

June Lockhart was of course familiar with the story, having starred in the movie *Son of Lassie*, and decided to make Ruth Martin more of an emancipated woman than her predecessor, capable of managing the farm and driving a pick-up truck. It was not long, either, before she was working more directly with Lassie than she had been in the film: 'The trainers used to stand on opposite sides of the set waving pieces of beef and calling the dog's name to get Lassie's head to turn just so. After a while you got so used to the technique that you never heard them calling the dog in between dialogue and then the sound editor simply cut it out.'

Lockhart, who was nominated for an Emmy in 1959 as Best Actress in a Continuing Character in a Dramatic Series, also tells one of the best stories about the extent to which the scriptwriters stretched Lassie's fabled intelligence.

**June Lockhart and Jon Provost, who co-starred in the television series for six years until the mid-1960s**

There was one scene where my car got a flat, and when I took the spare out it rolled down the hill. I chased it and got my foot stuck in a bear trap. At that moment Lassie showed up. I told her, 'Lassie, you know the C clamp that's on the counter beside the kitchen sink? Well, go bring it to me.' Lassie ran through the fields, opened the kitchen door, pulled something off the counter and ran back to drop it in my lap. And I said, 'No, Lassie, that's a cheese slicer. I said a C clamp!' and made a C with my hands. This time she fetched the right gadget and I got free.

Jon Prevost, another child actor best remembered for his role in the series, also recalls his time with Lassie with wry amusement.

Occasionally the dog needed a little encouragement to lick my face on cue. Sometimes Lassie would do it; sometimes he wouldn't, so they put a little butter on my face or a little tuna fish oil or something like that. After the first lick, he'd got all this makeup taste, so he wouldn't want to do it again unless they enticed him. The trainers always had to be on set. If I told Lassie to sit down or shake hands or something he would look at me and you could see him thinking, 'Wait a minute – you're not my trainer', and wait for his cue.

The actor also smiles when remembering how an expression frequently used by his screen mother, 'Yaseetimmee', became a catch phrase. He explains, 'At the end of every episode, June would have to sit me down and say, "You see, Timmy", and the phrase became a kind of moral lesson or social truth about humanity drawn from Lassie's exploits. It got used everywhere from comedy shows to political speeches!'

It was during the Ruth and Timmy era that the series became a big hit in the UK. An episode in November 1958, 'The Bundle from Britain', introduced Robin, an English relative of the Martins, who amused the rural American lads with his manner of speech and the fact that although he was thirteen years old he still wore short trousers. Unabashed, Robin (stoically played by a young American actor, Billy Potton) defended his clothes by explaining that his father had worn them at his age and it helped boys 'not to outgrow childhood too fast'. It was an explanation that must have made a lot of teenage boys on both sides of the Atlantic laugh aloud. There were some amusing scenes, too, between Lassie and Robin's little Cairn terrier Basil, who had apparently been able to visit America without any hold-up for quarantine.

Although *Lassie* always championed 'wholesome family values', the series occasionally became the target of attacks from parent groups monitoring its storylines. Some of these plots, with children being shown in danger of their lives, were branded 'unsuitable' for viewing at 7 p.m. on Sundays. There were others who maintained that Timmy's constant absences – although he was usually with Lassie – would encourage children to disobey their parents. Such attitudes, though, did little to halt the continuing success of the programme.

In 1964 Paul and Ruth Martin 'emigrated' to Australia, and, because Lassie could not go with them owing to 'animal control regulations' and Jon Provost was too old to play Timmy, the collie was left to continue his adventures with a neighbour, Cully Wilson (Andy Clyde, 1958–64) and then a Forest Ranger, Corey Stuart (Robert Bray, 1964–9). Later the canine star appeared on her own in many of the stories, demonstrating her prowess as a rescue dog and focusing attention on a number of topical environmental issues.

An attempt to reintroduce Lassie to cinema audiences was made in 1963 when director William Beaudine edited a five-part television serial, *The Journey*, into a single film, *Lassie's Great Adventure*. The story described how Timmy and Lassie survived being blown away in a balloon during a freak storm and then endured a long trek through the Canadian wilderness to reach home. If the release was not as popular as it might have been, audiences welcomed the chance to see Lassie in Technicolor – the television series would not be aired in colour for another two years.

A second attempt at combining episodes from television for the cinema was made in 1975 with *Lassie: Adventures of Neeka*. It took three 1969 stories, 'Night of the Ghost', 'Time of Crisis' and 'Price of Wisdom', and showed Lassie, now living with Forest Ranger Scott Turner (Jed Allan) in a California National Forest, rescue a headstrong young Aleut boy named Neeka (played by Mark Miranda) from various perils including drowning, a runaway truck and even a ghost town. Although dismissed by critics, the film has proved popular at film festivals.

A more successful adaptation was made in 1978 when Wrather Productions effectively revamped the original *Lassie Come Home* and included elements of the television series for *The Magic of Lassie*, which Don Chaffey directed. The scriptwriters, Jean Holloway and Richard M. Sherman, now had Lassie living in the Napa Valley with two orphaned children and their grandfather, who resists selling his land to a rich industrialist. In retaliation, the industrialist snatches Lassie from her home, and she has to make an arduous trek back over hundreds of mountainous miles to the valley and help her three friends save their property. The film was beautifully filmed at the Hop Kiln Winery in Healdsbury, northern California, with the wonderful veteran actor James Stewart as Clovis Mitchell and Michael Sharrett and Stephanie Zimbalist as his two grandchildren. The film was packed with songs, too – one of them, 'When You're Loved', being nominated for an Oscar – and proved popular with family audiences in America and Britain.

The same year a pilot for a new television series, *Lassie: A New Beginning*, also directed by Don Chaffey, was screened in two parts in September. The script by Jack Miller and Earl Hamner Jr – creator of the hugely popular television series *The Waltons* – put Lassie on the road yet again, accompanying two orphans,

The veteran James Stewart with Michael Sharrett and Stephanie Zimbalist in *The Magic of Lassie* (1978)

Samantha and Chip Stratton (Sally Boyden and Shane Sinutko), as they travelled from Arizona to southern California, hoping to find their only living relative and having to face one hazard after another that only Lassie could help them overcome. The ratings were poor, however, and no series was commissioned. Another decade passed before the collie reappeared on the screen.

It was not, in fact, until the end of the 1980s – with all the social upheaval that era brought – that an attempt was made to give the series a fresh start on air with *The New Lassie*, which was first broadcast in September 1989. The thirty-minute episodes produced by Al Burton and director Sigmund Neufeld Jr began with 'Lassie At Last', relocating the collie to Glenridge, California, where she lived with young Will McCullough (Will Estes), his sister Megan (Wendy Cox), their construction-worker father Chris (Christopher Stone) and his wife Dee (Dee Wallace Stone). With a nice touch of synergy, the grown-up Jon Provost, who had played Timmy, was hired for the first episode as Will's uncle, Steve. Once again Provost found Lassie coming to his rescue after he had been left shot and wounded by a deer hunter trapping out of season.

Jon Provost was not the only former member of the *Lassie* cast to appear in *The New Lassie*. Tommy Rettig, who had been retired from acting for years, was featured again as both writer and co-star of an episode entitled 'The Computer Studio'. The storyline drew on the actor's subsequent career as a software designer for universities and the US government, with Lassie using a computer helped by Tommy as a grown-up Jeff Miller. Like so many child stars who found adult roles hard to come by, Rettig had led a colourful life in the intervening years and attracted headlines for growing marijuana and allegedly being involved in drugs. He set the record straight talking to Brendan Bourne: 'The publicity people would rather not have marijuana and Lassie mentioned in the same paragraph. I was never in trouble with drugs. I had some trouble with the law in experimenting with drugs. I have never been an addict.' (Sadly, Tommy Rettig died of heart failure just four years later in 1996.)

June Lockhart, who had played Ruth Miller for six years, also guested in another episode of *The New Lassie* with a nice acknowledgement to the past entitled 'Roots'. Fans with long memories were similarly delighted to see Roddy McDowall from the original *Lassie Come Home* co-star in no fewer than three episodes, 'Guess Who's Coming to Breakfast, Lunch and Dinner?' 'Leeds, the Judge' and 'A Will and a Way'.

The series also deserves credit for providing the screen début of a young actor who is now one of the world's most famous film stars. Leonardo DiCaprio was trying to get a start in show business in the autumn of 1990 when he was offered a role in the aptly titled episode 'Livewire'. He was one of a group of young baseball players whose field is threatened by the fall of a power line that electrifies a fence and will kill anyone who touches it – not, though, before the usual last-minute intervention by Lassie. Not even the appearance of this superstar-in-the-making could save *The New Lassie* from being dropped after a commendable fifty-one episodes in September 1991.

In 1994 scriptwriter Matthew Jacobs was given the opportunity to go right back to the original wellspring of Eric Knight's original story in order to reintroduce Lassie to yet another new generation. Updated and set in West Virginia, *Lassie* – with the tag line, 'Best Friends Are Forever' – featured Matt Turner (Tom Guiry), a lad in total contrast to his progenitor Sam Carraclough half a century earlier. Tom is a typical disaffected city kid more interested in his skateboard and Walkman than the new ranch home in the countryside to which his recently widowed father Steve (Jon Tenney) is taking him. On their way the pair come

**On location in West Virginia in 1994 for *Lassie* – 'Best Friends Are Forever'**

across a fatal car accident from which the only survivor is a collie dog who promptly attaches himself to Matt. The uniting of dog and teenager proves the precursor to a new and happier life for them both. Older members of the audience were no doubt amused by the in-jokes inserted by director Daniel Petrie, notably Matt's dislike of reruns of the *Lassie* series on television and his refusal to believe that the dog the Turners have found *is* the famous collie!

During the 1970s there had also been another reinvention of Lassie as an animated cartoon character. In 1975 Filmation launched a television series, *Lassie's Rescue Rangers*, directed by Hal Sutherland, which ran for two years. This time the collie was the leader of a team of rescuers who included the Turner

**Lassie makes her début in yet another new medium, the animated cartoon, in _Lassie's Rescue Rangers_ (1975)**

family – Ben, Laura, Jackie and Susan – as well as a motley band of comic animal characters including Robbie (a raccoon), Fastback (a turtle), Edgar (a crow), Musty (a skunk) and Old Toothless (a mountain lion). The series began with 'Lassie and the Spirit of Thunder Mountain' and continued with episodes of a similar nature that ranged across the continent, such as 'The Mystic Monster', 'Deepsea Disaster', 'Arctic Adventure' and 'Hullabaloo in Hollywood'. Ted Knight, Jane Webb, Keith Sutherland and Lane Scheimer provided the voices. In 2004 the programme was repeated on ABC as _Lassie the Super Collie_.

The Japanese, who have been fans of the Lassie films and television series for many years, added their own contribution in 1996 with the animated _Meiken_

*Rasshi* (*Famous Dog Lassie*). Produced by Nippon Animation and directed by Katabuchi Sunao, the series introduced Lassie as a pup found at the roadside by a young lad, John. The collie becomes devoted to the boy and his family and helps them overcome various social and domestic dramas. Artistic creator Morikawa Soko drew a more puppy-like Lassie, obviously with small children and the soft-toy market in mind, although his animation has been praised for its attention to detail, facial expressions and animal movements. The evocative opening theme song, 'Owaranai Monogatari' ('Endless Story'), hinted that even when the series came to an end after twenty-five episodes the legend of Lassie had still far from run its course. Indeed, at the time of writing, a major movie remake of the original *Lassie Come Home* is being filmed by director and producer Charles Sturridge, with Peter O'Toole in the role of the Duke of Rudling, Samantha Morton playing Sarah Carraclough and with Peter Dinklage as Rowlie. A strong supporting cast includes Steve Pemberton, John Lynch, Jemma Redgrave and Gregor Fisher. Locations include Ireland and the Isle of Man.

It seems that the image of a boy calling, 'Here, girl!' to the world's quadruped sweetheart as they set off on yet another adventure is as compelling now as it has always been.

In the title role: Carter the collie on the set of Charles Sturridge's film *Lassie* at Kilruddery House, Ireland, 2005 (photograph: Haydn West/PA/EMPICS)

A 1949 publicity shot for *The Courage of Lassie* (LP Pics)